Cool Middle Eastern Cooking

Fun and Tasty Recipes for Kids

Lisa Wagner

TO ADULT HELPERS

You're invited to assist an up-and-coming chef! As children learn to cook, they develop new skills, gain confidence, and make some delicious food. What's more, it's going to be a lot of fun!

Efforts have been made to keep the recipes in this book authentic yet simple. You will notice that some of the recipes are more difficult than others. Be there to help children with these recipes, but encourage them to do as much as they can on their own. Also encourage them to try new foods and experiment with their own ideas. Building creativity into the cooking process encourages children to think like real chefs.

Before getting started, set some ground rules about using the kitchen, cooking tools, and ingredients. Most importantly, adult supervision is a must whenever a child uses the stove, oven, or sharp tools.

So, put on your aprons and stand by. Let your young chefs take the lead. Watch and learn. Taste their creations. Praise their efforts. Enjoy the culinary adventure!

visit us at www.abdopublishing.com

Published by ABDO Publishing Company, a division of ABDO, P.O. Box 398166, Minneapolis, Minnesota 55439. Copyright © 2011 by Abdo Consulting Group, Inc. International copyrights reserved in all countries. No part of this book may be reproduced in any form without written permission from the publisher. Checkerboard Library™ is a trademark and logo of ABDO Publishing Company.

Printed in the United States of America, North Mankato, Minnesota
102010
012011

 PRINTED ON RECYCLED PAPER

Design and Production: Colleen Dolphin, Mighty Media, Inc.
Art Direction: Colleen Dolphin
Series Editor: Liz Salzmann
Food Production: Frankie Tuminelly
Photo Credits: Colleen Dolphin, Photodisc, Shutterstock

The following manufacturers/names appearing in this book are trademarks: Arrowhead Mills®, Betty Crocker®, Fage®, Gold Medal®, Krinos Foods, Inc.®, La Preferida®, Market Pantry®, Morton®, Oster® Osterizer®, Pyrex®, Target®

Library of Congress Cataloging-in-Publication Data

Wagner, Lisa, 1958-
  Cool Middle Eastern cooking : fun and tasty recipes for kids / Lisa Wagner.
     p. cm. -- (Cool world cooking)
  Includes index.
  ISBN 978-1-61714-663-3
  1. Cooking, Middle Eastern--Juvenile literature. I. Title.
  TX725.M628W34 2011
  641.5956--dc22
                              2010022195

Table of Contents

Explore the Foods of the Middle East

The Middle East is often called the cradle of civilization. People have lived there for more than 7,000 years! During this long history, recipes have been shared between many different people.

Today, many countries are informally a part of the Middle East. Most are in Asia near the Mediterranean Sea. This book includes recipes from Israel, Lebanon, Turkey, and Greece. Greece isn't always considered part of the Middle East. But Greek cooking includes many of the same ingredients and flavors!

Middle Eastern dishes often include nuts, olives, rice, and wheat. Chicken and lamb are the most popular meats. Yogurt and goat cheese are common too. Cinnamon, cumin, cayenne pepper, and paprika are popular spices. Are you ready for a tasty Middle Eastern adventure? Put on your apron, and off we go!

GET THE PICTURE!

When a step number in a recipe
has a dotted circle around it, look
for the picture that goes with it.
The circle around the photo will be
the same color as the step number.

4 →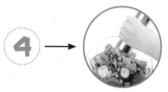

HOW DO YOU SAY THAT?

You may come across some Middle
Eastern words you've never heard
of in this book. Don't worry! There's
a pronunciation guide on page 30!

The Basics

Get going in the right direction
with a few important basics!

ASK PERMISSION

Before you cook, get permission to
use the kitchen, cooking tools, and
ingredients. When you need help,
ask. Always get help when you use
the stove or oven.

GET ORGANIZED

- Being well organized is a chef's secret
  ingredient for success!

- Read through the entire recipe before
  you do anything else.

- Gather all your cooking tools and
  ingredients.

- Get the ingredients ready. The list
  of ingredients tells how to prepare
  each item.

- Put each prepared ingredient into
  a separate bowl.

- Read the recipe instructions carefully.
  Do the steps in the order they are listed.

GOOD COOKING TAKES PREP WORK

Many ingredients need preparation
before they are used. Look at a recipe's
ingredients list. Some ingredients will
have words such as chopped, sliced, or
grated next to them. These words tell
you how to prepare the ingredients.

Give yourself plenty of time and
be patient. Always wash fruits and
vegetables. Rinse them well and pat
them dry with a **towel**. Then they
won't slip when you cut them. After
you prepare each ingredient, put it in a
separate prep bowl. Now you're ready!

BE SMART, BE SAFE

- If you use the stove or oven, you need an adult with you.

- Never use the stove or oven if you are home alone.

- Always get an adult to help with the hot jobs, such as frying with oil.

- Have an adult nearby when you are using sharp tools such as knives, peelers, graters, or food processors.

- Always turn pot handles to the back of the stove. This helps prevent accidents and spills.

- Work slowly and carefully. If you get hurt, let an adult know right away!

BE NEAT, BE CLEAN

- Start with clean hands, clean tools, and a clean work surface.

- Tie back long hair so it stays out of the way and out of the food.

- Roll up your sleeves.

- An apron will protect your clothes from spills and splashes.

- Chef hats are **optional!**

KEY SYMBOLS

In this book, you will see some symbols beside the recipes. Here is what they mean.

HOT STUFF!
The recipe requires the use of a stove or oven. You need adult assistance and supervision.

SUPER SHARP!
A sharp tool such as a peeler, knife, or grater is needed. Get an adult to stand by.

NUT ALERT!
Some people can get very sick if they eat nuts. If you are cooking with nuts, let people know!

EVEN COOLER!
This symbol means adventure! Give it a try! Get inspired and invent your own cool ideas.

No Germs Allowed!

Raw eggs and raw meat have bacteria in them. These bacteria are killed when food is cooked. But they can survive out in the open and make you sick! After you handle raw eggs or meat, wash your hands, tools, and work surfaces with soap and water. Keep everything clean!

The Tool Box

A box on the bottom of the first page of each recipe lists the tools you need.
When you come across a tool you don't know, turn back to these pages.

SERRATED KNIFE

SMALL SHARP KNIFE

CUTTING BOARD

MEASURING CUPS

MEASURING SPOONS

LIQUID MEASURING CUP

PREP BOWLS

MIXING BOWLS

WOODEN SPOON

WHISK

PASTRY BRUSH

SPOON

SPATULA

CAN OPENER

FORK

PEELER

PAPER TOWELS

PLASTIC WRAP

TIMER

SAUCEPAN

SERVING BOWLS

STRAINER

SALAD BOWL

FRYING PAN

PEPPER GRINDER

POT HOLDERS

GRATER

JUICER

BLENDER

9 × 9-INCH BAKING DISH

WIRE BAKING RACK

ROUND GLASS BAKING DISH

Cool Cooking Terms

Here are some basic cooking terms and the actions that go with them. Whenever you need a reminder, just turn back to these pages.

FIRST THINGS FIRST

Always wash fruit and vegetables well. Rinse them under cold water. Pat them dry with a **towel**. Then they won't slip when you cut them.

CHOP

Chop means to cut things into small pieces with a knife.

CUBE OR DICE

Cube and *dice* mean to cut cube or dice shapes. Usually *dice* refers to smaller pieces and *cube* refers to larger pieces.

GRATE

Grate means to shred something into small pieces using a grater.

MIX

Mix means to stir ingredients together, usually with a large spoon.

WHISK

Whisk means to beat quickly by hand with a whisk or fork.

SLICE

Slice means to cut food into pieces of the same thickness.

MINCE

Mince means to cut the food into the tiniest possible pieces. Garlic is often minced.

BLEND

Blend means to mix ingredients together with a blender.

PEEL

Peel means to remove the skin, often with a peeler.

JUICE

To *juice* a fruit means to remove the juice from its insides by squeezing it or using a juicer.

The Coolest Ingredients

TOMATO

WHITE ONION

POTATOES

LEMONS

CARROTS

RADISHES

GARLIC

LETTUCE

GREEN PEPPER

FRESH PARSLEY

FRESH OREGANO

FRESH MINT

SCALLIONS

PITA BREAD

SALT

CUCUMBER

GROUND CINNAMON

GROUND CUMIN

WALNUTS

PAPRIKA

GROUND PEPPER

13

ALL-PURPOSE FLOUR

BULGUR WHEAT

CHICKEN BROTH

LONG-GRAIN RICE

GROUND BEEF

CHICKEN BREASTS

CHICKPEAS

TAHINI

GREEK YOGURT

EGG

BUTTER

SUGAR

Olive oil bottle

OLIVE OIL

SEMISWEET CHOCOLATE CHIPS

Milk

MILK

HONEY

PIE CRUST MIX

Allergy Alert!

Some people have a reaction when they eat certain foods. If you have any allergies, you know what it's all about. An allergic reaction can require emergency **medical** help. Nut allergies can be especially **dangerous**. Before you serve anything made with nuts or peanut oil, ask if anyone has a nut allergy.

Salt and Pepper to Taste?

Some recipes say to add salt and pepper to taste. This means you should rely on your taste buds. Take a small spoonful of the food and taste it. If it isn't as salty as you like, add a little salt. If it needs more ground pepper, add some. Then mix and taste it again.

Middle Eastern Extras

Take your Middle Eastern cooking to the next level! The ideas on these pages will show you how.

TEMPTING TZATZIKI SAUCE

Makes 2 cups

INGREDIENTS
2 cucumbers, peeled, seeded, and diced
2 cups Greek yogurt
2 cloves garlic, minced
½ teaspoon salt
juice from 1 lemon
1 tablespoon dried or fresh mint
¼ cup olive oil (**optional**)

1 Mix all ingredients together.

2 Chill for at least 1 hour before serving.

SIMPLE RICE PILAF

Makes 4 to 6 servings

INGREDIENTS
2 tablespoons butter
1 cup long-grain rice
1 teaspoon salt
2½ cups chicken broth

1 Melt the butter in a frying pan over medium-high heat. Add the rice and salt.

2 Stir constantly for about 2 minutes. The rice should start to turn golden and the butter should get foamy.

3 Slowly add the broth and stir. Bring to a boil over medium heat.

4 Cover the frying pan. Turn the heat to the lowest setting. Simmer for 25 to 30 minutes until the liquid is **absorbed**. Take the pan off the heat. Let it sit, covered, for 15 minutes. Stir the rice before serving.

CLASSIC HUMMUS DIP

Makes about 1½ cups

INGREDIENTS

1 15 oz can chickpeas, rinsed and drained
¼ cup tahini
2-3 cloves garlic, chopped (**optional**)
½ teaspoon salt
juice from 1 lemon
⅓ cup olive oil
1 tablespoon water
paprika

1 Put all the ingredients except the paprika in a blender. Blend until very smooth.

2 Put the hummus in a serving bowl. Sprinkle it with paprika. Serve with cut vegetables or pita bread.

LEBANESE TAHINA

Makes about 2 cups

INGREDIENTS

2 cloves garlic, minced
1 teaspoon salt
¾ cup tahini
½ cup lemon juice
1 cup water
paprika
2 tablespoons chopped fresh parsley

1 Mix the garlic and salt together with a wooden spoon until it becomes a paste.

2 Mix in the tahini and the lemon juice.

3 Add the water slowly. Whisk until the mixture is smooth. If you like a thinner sauce, add more lemon juice and water.

4 Sprinkle the top with paprika and parsley before serving.

Harriet's Tasty Tabbouleh

This Lebanese salad is healthy and oh, so tasty!

MAKES 6 TO 8 SERVINGS

INGREDIENTS

2 cups water

¾ cup bulgur wheat

2 large bunches of parsley, finely chopped

1 cup finely chopped fresh mint

½ bunch scallions, finely chopped

2 large tomatoes, finely chopped

1 small dried onion, finely chopped

⅔ cup fresh lemon juice

½ cup olive oil

salt and pepper to taste

TOOLS:
prep bowls
measuring cups
cutting board

serrated knife
small sharp knife
juicer

saucepan
strainer
mixing bowls

whisk
wooden spoon

1. Boil the water in a saucepan. Turn off the heat and stir in the bulgur wheat. Let it stand for 30 minutes.

2. Rinse the bulgur wheat in strainer. Then drain and squeeze excess water out. Put it in a large mixing bowl. Add the parsley, mint, scallions, tomatoes, and dried onions. Mix well.

3. Whisk the olive oil and lemon juice together in a small bowl. Pour it over the bulgur wheat mixture.

4. Mix well. Add salt and pepper to taste.

Even Cooler!

For a more **authentic** tabbouleh, add ½ teaspoon ground cinnamon and increase parsley to 3 cups. Or spice it up and add ¼ teaspoon cayenne pepper.

Crispy Crunchy Veggie Salad

A delicious Israeli salad
full of garden-fresh flavors!

MAKES 6 TO 8 SERVINGS

TOOLS:

prep bowls	small sharp knife	salad bowl	spoon	pepper grinder
cutting board	measuring cups	mixing bowl	forks	juicer
serrated knife	measuring spoons	whisk	peeler	

1 Put the tomatoes and all the vegetables in a **salad** bowl.

2 Whisk together the olive oil and lemon juice to make the dressing.

3 Pour the dressing over the vegetables. Use two forks to toss the salad. Add parsley and mix well.

4 Grind pepper over the top, then mix to blend. Add salt and pepper to taste. Chill for at least 1 hour before serving.

Even Cooler!

Make a Greek salad instead. **Omit** the radishes and carrots. Use 1 small red onion instead of the scallions. Slice the onion into thin wedges. Add ¼ cup pitted Kalamata olives. Crumble 2 ounces of feta cheese over the top before serving.

Tip

To peel and seed a cucumber, remove the peel with a vegetable peeler. Cut the cucumber in half the long way. Then use a spoon to scrape away the seeds.

Turkish Kofta Creations

This delightful Turkish favorite is just the thing for lunch or dinner!

MAKES 8 SERVINGS

INGREDIENTS

- 2 lb. ground beef
- ½ cup finely chopped fresh parsley
- ¼ cup finely chopped fresh mint
- 1 medium onion, grated
- 2 teaspoons ground cumin
- 1 teaspoon ground cinnamon
- 1 teaspoon salt
- ½ teaspoon ground pepper
- ¼ cup olive oil
- pita bread, cut in half
- onion, thinly sliced
- tomatoes, sliced
- lettuce
- tzatziki (see page 16)

TOOLS:

prep bowls	cutting board	mixing bowl
measuring cups	small sharp knife	frying pan
measuring spoons	grater	spatula

1. Put the meat, parsley, mint, and grated onion in a mixing bowl. Mix with your hands. Make sure to wash them first! Add the cumin, cinnamon, salt, pepper, and olive oil. Mix well.

2. Divide the meat mixture into 16 equal portions. Roll each portion into a ball. Flatten each ball slightly to make a patty.

3. Put a little olive oil in a frying pan. Heat the oil over medium high heat. Add several patties. Fry them for 3 minutes on each side. Add more olive oil to the frying pan before cooking the remaining patties.

4. Serve the kofta patties on pita bread with sliced onion, tomatoes, lettuce, and tzatziki.

Even Cooler!

You can bake the kofta patties instead of frying them. Preheat the oven to 350 degrees. Put the kofta patties on a baking sheet. Bake for 12 to 15 minutes, until cooked all the way through.

Golden Potato Latkes

INGREDIENTS

4 medium potatoes, peeled

1 onion (about 2 inches across), grated

3 tablespoons all-purpose flour

½ teaspoon salt

1 egg, beaten

olive oil

Make a great meal with this Israeli specialty and applesauce!

MAKES 8 CAKES

TOOLS: prep bowls   measuring spoons   strainer   spatula
peeler   measuring cups   mixing bowl   paper towels
grater   fork   frying pan

1 Grate the potatoes using the largest holes on the grater. Put the potatoes in a strainer and press out the moisture. The potatoes hold a lot of moisture. Use your hands to squeeze out as much as you can.

2 Put the potatoes in a large bowl. Add the grated onion and mix with a fork. Add the flour, salt, and beaten egg. Mix well.

3 Heat ¼ inch of oil in a heavy frying pan over medium-high heat. After a few minutes, test the oil. Add a teaspoon of the potato mixture. If it starts to sizzle and brown right away, the oil is ready.

4 Put ⅓ cup of the potato mixture into the oil. Flatten it with a spatula to about ½ inch thick. Slip the spatula under the latke to keep it from sticking to the bottom of the frying pan. Fry 3 to 4 minutes until you see the edges turning golden brown.

5 Turn the latke over very carefully so the hot oil doesn't splash. Fry 3 to 4 minutes on the other side. Both sides should be golden brown. Put the latke on paper **towels** to drain.

6 Repeat Steps 4 and 5 to make more latkes. Serve them warm with applesauce or sour cream.

Greek Herbed Chicken

The simple Greek marinade makes the best-tasting chicken ever!

MAKES 4 TO 6 SERVINGS

INGREDIENTS

- ⅓ cup lemon juice
- ⅔ cup olive oil
- 4 cloves garlic, minced
- ¼ cup chopped fresh oregano
- 2 tablespoons chopped fresh parsley
- 1 teaspoon salt
- ½ teaspoon ground pepper
- 1 lb. chicken breasts, cut into serving pieces

TOOLS: whisk
prep bowls
juicer
measuring cups

measuring spoons
cutting board
small sharp knife
mixing bowls

wooden spoon
9 x 9-inch baking dish
plastic wrap

pot holders
timer

1. Put the lemon juice, olive oil, and garlic in a small bowl. Whisk them together. Add the oregano, parsley, salt, and pepper and mix. This is the **marinade**.

2. Put the chicken pieces in a large bowl. Pour the marinade over chicken.

3. Mix to coat the chicken evenly with the marinade. Cover the bowl with plastic wrap. Refrigerate for at least two hours and up to 24 hours. Preheat the oven to 400 degrees.

4. Put the chicken and marinade into 9 x 9-inch baking dish. Bake for 30 minutes. Turn the oven down to 350 degrees. Bake for 30 to 45 minutes until chicken is cooked through. To check whether the chicken is done, cut into a thick piece. If it is not pink inside, the chicken is done.

Even Cooler!

Add other herbs to the marinade. Thyme and rosemary are good choices. Use 1 tablespoon of each. You can add up to 3 extra herbs.

Nummy Nut Wedges

A sweet and scrumptious Greek treat made with honey!

MAKES 8 TO 10 SERVINGS

INGREDIENTS

1 package pie crust mix (for 2 crusts)

½ cup sugar

3 to 4 tablespoons water

flour

1 cup walnuts, finely chopped

2 tablespoons honey

1 teaspoon ground cinnamon

1 teaspoon lemon juice

milk

½ cup semisweet chocolate pieces

1 teaspoon butter

TOOLS: prep bowls, measuring cups, measuring spoons, juicer, small sharp knife, cutting board, mixing bowls, spoon, round pie dish, fork, pastry brush, wire rack, small saucepan

1 Preheat the oven to 375 degrees.

2 In a medium bowl stir together pie crust mix and ¼ cup sugar. Add enough water to form a ball of dough. Divide the dough in half.

3 Sprinkle a little flour onto the counter. Roll each half of the dough into a 9-inch circle. Put one of the circles on an ungreased round pie dish.

4 Combine the nuts, ¼ cup sugar, honey, cinnamon, and lemon juice in a bowl.

5 Spread the nut mixture over the dough on the round pie dish. Put the other dough circle on top.

6 Use the tines of a fork to press around the edges of the dough.

7 Prick the top of the dough with a fork. Brush it with milk. Bake for 15 to 20 minutes or until **pastry** starts to brown. Put the pie on a wire rack.

8 Combine the chocolate pieces and butter in a small saucepan. Cook and stir over low heat just until melted. Drizzle the chocolate over the warm pie. Cut the pie into eight to ten wedges. Let them cool completely before serving.

Wrap it Up!

Now you know how to make **delicious** Middle Eastern dishes! What did you learn? Did you try any new foods? Learning about recipes from around the world teaches you a lot. You learn about different **cultures**, climates, geography, and tastes.

Making international dishes also teaches you about different languages. Did you learn any new words in this book? These new words will help you sound like a native speaker. They'll come in handy at restaurants and **grocery stores**.

Bulgur (BUL-gur)

Hummus (HUHM-uhss)

Kofta (KOHF-tah)

Latke (LAHT-kuh)

Pilaf (PEE-lof)

Tabbouleh (tuh-BOO-luh)

Tahini (tuh-HEE-nee)

Tzatziki (tsah-TSEE-kee)

Glossary

absorb – to soak up or take in.

authentic – real or true.

culture – the behavior, beliefs, art, and other products of a particular group of people.

dangerous – able or likely to cause harm or injury.

delicious – very pleasing to taste or smell.

grocery store – a place where you buy food items.

marinade – a sauce that food is soaked in before cooking.

medical – having to do with doctors or the science of medicine.

omit – to leave out.

optional – something you can choose, but is not required.

pastry – dough used to make pies and other baked goods.

salad – a mixture of raw vegetables usually served with a dressing.

towel – a cloth or paper used for cleaning or drying.

Web Sites

To learn more about cool cooking, visit ABDO Publishing Company on the World Wide Web at **www.abdopublishing. com.** Web sites about cool cooking are featured on our Book Links page. These links are routinely monitored and updated to provide the most current information available.

Index